Princess Victoria's eighteenth birthday was celebrated on 24th May 1837, less than a month before her accession to the throne. The Birmingham medallist Thomas Halliday captured the spirit of the coming age by depicting the princess as ENGLAND'S OPENING ROSE. *(Actual size 1½ inches, 38 mm, diameter).*

VICTORIAN SOUVENIR MEDALS

Daniel Fearon

Shire Publications Ltd

737. 222_094.1
FEA

CONTENTS

Set in 9 point Times roman and printed in Great Britain by C. I. Thomas and Sons (Haverfordwest) Ltd, Press Buildings, Merlins Bridge, Haverfordwest, Dyfed.

British Library Cataloguing in Publication Data available.

ACKNOWLEDGEMENTS

I most gratefully acknowledge the kindness of Spink and Son for allowing me to photograph a selection of white metal medals. My thanks go to Mr Stan Kaluza for the loan of, and advice on, medals of railways and bridges, and similarly to Mr Bernard Myers for architectural medals. The medal of Hermit is reproduced by kind permission of the Trustees of the British Museum. All the remaining medals come from one further collection and the owner, who wishes to remain anonymous, is no less gratefully acknowledged. The photography is by Charles Nickols and Piak Latchford.

NOTE

With the exception of the medal on page 1 all medals are shown actual size. Except where only one face is shown, the medals are illustrated with the obverse on the left and the reverse on the right.

COVER: *A selection of white metal medals displayed with a small Victorian collector's cabinet. A Jubilee medal of 1897 is shown with its original box and an advertising leaflet.*

BELOW: *Ribands for suspending badges and medals, advertised in the Spink's catalogue. Plain riband 1¼ inches (30 mm) wide cost 12s 6d for 36 yards (32.9 m), striped riband cost 14s 6d for the same length and narrow riband only 1s 9d.*

Queen Victoria was crowned on 28th June 1838. On this medal by T. W. Ingram the head has been copied from the proposed coinage portrait.

INTRODUCTION

The fashion for the cheap souvenir medal was established long before Queen Victoria came to the throne in 1837. The Birmingham manufactories had followed the lead given them by Matthew Boulton, but whereas he is famous for a range of high-quality medals in copper or precious metals his followers turned to mass production. They soon perfected a bright silvery alloy and struck what was, in substance, a tin medal, but with a superior and rich-looking surface. The inventor of the metal named it, with considerable lack of imagination, *white metal.* White metal medals were inexpensive to make, the metal was soft and easy to strike and the bright surface gave the medallist plenty of scope for a fine array of designs. As many gold, silver and copper medals were produced as had been before, but during the last years of the reign of George III and during the reigns of George IV and William IV the growing use of white metal enabled more and more events to be commemorated with a struck medal.

On the medal struck for her eighteenth birthday, on 24th May 1837, Princess Victoria was hailed as ENGLAND'S OPENING ROSE. In less than a month, on 20th June, she succeeded to the throne. White metal medals recorded the succession and over the next 63 years of Victoria's reign white metal medals commemorated people and events great and small. Those which survive, though often overlooked or ignored, provide a fascinating record of the Victorian age. They are captivating pieces, some of them now scarce and a few probably very rare, which are always enjoyable and eminently collectable.

Whilst there is obvious delight in handling the medals, it is curious how little is known about the ways the Victorian manufacturers marketed and sold them. How indeed did the public buy them? Or simply who bought them? Some were made as free 'give-away' souvenirs, but others were bought by individuals or organisations. Late in the reign, the London coin and medal dealers Spink and Son published amazing brochures for their medals of the Diamond Jubilee of Queen Victoria — all of which showed a distinctive bust of the Queen, designed by Frank Bowcher — and 'not the rubbish usually offered to the public on these occasions, but ... from finely executed dies, and of superior finish.' Elaborate forms with a page of codes for bulk ordering by telegraphic cable, were inserted in the brochures and the prices *were* cheap. Today, perhaps, it is easier to understand the cheapness, but the sheer volume of varieties offered for sale seems to be endless. Orders were taken for special designs, so that a local organisation could have a medal struck with the standard obverse of the Queen, but their own reverse. The cost for a single 1½ inch (38 mm) medal die — the cheapest — was £2 10s.

The brochures are an extraordinary record, for the most expensive white metal medal, 3 inches (76 mm) in diameter, with a reverse symbolic of the British Empire, was only 5 shillings, and the price included a leather case. A 'special cheap medal for little children' sold at 7s 6d for a box of forty-eight, each with a neck ribbon — less than tuppence each. There seemed to be about as many varieties of ribbons and metal suspenders, for wearing the medals, as there were actual medals, and the ribbons, too, came in different grades.

The collector of white metal medals need not be worried by any possible eccentricities of the numismatic world, for commemorative medals are by their nature self-explanatory and carry the details of the person or event they commemorate. The traditional Latin legend that was commonplace on the medals of the previous 250 years was replaced by English words everyone could understand. White metal medals were sometimes commissioned, though many were struck by private enterprise for commercial reasons. They were not the official issues of government or royal command, so the designs were free from the multitude of restrictions that officialdom might place upon them. Individually, white metal souvenir medals are of local, personal or historical interest: collectively they are a delightful record of the age.

ROYALTY

When Queen Victoria came to the throne in 1837 she was eighteen years old and unmarried. Throughout her reign white metal medals recorded the events of her personal life: her Coronation, her marriage, the birth of her children, the death of Prince Albert, the marriages of her children and grandchildren, her Golden and Diamond Jubilees, and her death. It is medals marking these family events that are here termed royal, for royal portraits abound on many white metal medals commemorating openings, visits and other public occasions. Those medals are discussed later and indeed the collector of medals with royal portraits will often find that some of the best are found on very ordinary, and strictly commemorative, pieces.

The medal for Princess Victoria's eighteenth birthday was quickly followed by medals for her accession and, better still for the medallists, for the Coronation on 28th June 1838. The official Coronation medal by Benedetto Pistrucci (not struck in white metal) had been strongly criticised, but the commercial medallists simply churned out their products. As the medals were struck well in advance of the event, they could not record the cere-

mony itself and designs are full of symbolism: the kingdoms of England, Scotland and Ireland are personified, cornucopias overflow and justice, commerce, art, fame and genius are represented.

Victoria married Prince Albert of Saxe-Coburg and Gotha on 10th February 1840 and the medallists seem to have stayed within the accepted bounds of traditional marriage medals, showing on the obverse conjoined portrait busts of the couple, the Queen always to the fore. Reverse designs range from crowned shields of arms to symbolised and actual marriage blessings. The birth of Princess Victoria Adelaide Louisa, the Princess Royal, on 21st November 1840, was apparently deemed to be uncommercial, although the medallists dutifully recorded her christening the following February. Celebrating the birth of the future king was clearly more profitable and medals were struck when the Prince of Wales was born on 9th November 1841. Some ten years later the medallists Allen and Moore portrayed him in a sailor suit with the legend above reading BRITAIN'S HOPE. It was probably a souvenir sold at the Great Exhibition of 1851.

The Dowager Queen Adelaide, widow

A small medal for the birth of the Princess Royal in November 1840.

Victoria's coronation medals ranged from some quite grand designs to others, such as this, of a far more humble nature.

The use of a common obverse was an obvious economy, as on these medals for the marriage of Queen Victoria to Prince Albert (right), in 1840 and for the baptism of the Princess Royal in 1841 (below).

of William IV, died on 2nd December 1849 and a modest memorial medal bears the words BELOVED AND LAMENTED. The marriage, in 1858, of the Princess Royal to Prince Frederick William of Prussia was the subject of several medals, one even stating that it took place AT THE CHAPEL ROYAL SAINT JAMES'S. The birth of their son, the future Kaiser William II, does not seem to have been the subject of any British medal. The death of Prince

Albert, on 14th December 1861, was featured on a number of medals: most of the portraits are good, but reverse designs of weeping Britannias seem ill designed and purely sentimental. However, for such an unexpected event, the medallist would have to have acted quickly to get his product into the shops and standard designs would have been used.

The marriage of the Prince of Wales to Princess Alexandra of Denmark, on 10th

Marriage medals feature throughout the reign; this medal commemorates the marriage of the Princess Royal to Prince Frederick William of Prussia in 1858.

The marriage of Albert Edward, Prince of Wales, to Princess Alexandra of Denmark in 1863 was widely celebrated and the subject of many medals. This is by Ottley of Birmingham.

An unsigned medal also struck for the marriage of the Prince and Princess of Wales.

A later marriage medal was for Prince George, Duke of York, and Princess May of Teck in 1893 — later George V and Queen Mary.

March 1863, was a cause of much public rejoicing and the first excuse since the death of Prince Albert to commemorate a royal event with a medal, and happy events are always the most commercial. Less likely to catch the public imagination were the medals struck in 1872 to commemorate the Prince of Wales's recover from illness and the service of thanksgiving held at St Paul's Cathedral in London. Prince George, Duke of York (George V), became second in line to the throne following the death of his elder brother Prince Albert, in 1892. On 6th July 1893 his marriage to Princess May of Teck (who had been engaged to his brother) was commemorated with a number of medals.

As the Queen grew older the opportunities for striking royal medals dimi-

Prince Albert died in 1861, BELOVED and LAMENTED and the subject of many medals, many, such as this by J. Moore of Birmingham, showing a weeping Britannia.

The Prince of Wales had nearly died of typhoid fever in December 1871, but in February 1872 he went with the Queen to a national service of thanksgiving in St Paul's Cathedral. This medal, with its 'photographic' portrait, is by Ottley.

The jubilees of 1887 and 1897 brought a huge output of souvenir medals. Frank Bowcher designed a whole range for Spink and Son, some in white metal, such as this, and in other metals too.

Many of the best portraits of Victoria and Prince Albert occur on medals for events other than royal ones: these (showing obverses) were made by Ottley for the 1862 International Exhibition in London.

nished but there were two outstanding exceptions. In 1887, at the age of 68, the Queen celebrated her Golden Jubilee with much pomp and ceremony, and cheap souvenir medals, often with red, white and blue ribbons and suspension pins, were an important part of the festivites. Ten years later people sensed that the Diamond Jubilee would be her last and the quantity of medals struck must have far exceeded that of 1887. Throughout the British Isles towns and cities had medals struck to commemorate the event. Some were given to those present at civic receptions, others were given to schoolchildren. Frank Bowcher's well modelled head of the Queen, on a medal for Spink and Son selling for 9d (with a special price for a gross or more), was then, and remains, the most familiar of all these. The last of the royal medals commemorates the death of Queen Victoria on 22nd January 1901, a sad occasion recorded on only two or three different white metal medals.

PERSONALITIES

One of the great joys of the Victorian white metal medals is their variety. The personalities depicted on medals include the great men and women of the age, those who enjoyed a brief moment of fame on the fringe of history, and yet others who have been totally forgotten. Many great events and achievements centre around an individual who caught the imagination of the public and was then depicted on a simple souvenir medal.

News was not so instant then as it is now and it was certainly not so visual, therefore the portrait on the medal had an important role in making the public aware of the appearance of the personality upon it. As the nineteenth century progressed there was a notable increase in the number of full faces and three-quarter profiles, a type of portrait made easier by copying from photographs. The standard profile bust did not disappear, but it was no longer *de rigueur*. Even though the medals were intended as cheap souvenirs, and sometimes just hand-outs, the standard of the portraits on them was always high. There seem to have been no rules as to who qualified to appear on a cheap medal, but some of the more famous people of the age are found only on medals made of bronze and silver. Towards the end of Victoria's reign certain medals, such as Frank Bowcher's medals of Lord Roberts and Baden Powell struck by Spink and Son, were made in several metals, including white metal as the cheapest range.

The Duke of Wellington became as eminent a statesman as he had been a general, and when the new Royal Exchange was opened in 1844 his statue was erected outside. The statue and the £2,000 raised for it by public subscription are both recorded on souvenir medals bearing his distinctive profile. Many more medals were struck to commemorate his death in 1852. Daniel O'Connell, the first Irish Catholic member of Parliament, appears on a patriotic medal, struck two years before the Repeal of the Union in 1843, by the Dublin medallist W. Woodhouse. The four champions of the Anti-Corn Law League, William Cobden, John Bright, Pelham Villiers and Wilson are shown as the representatives of Free Trade, with the passing of the Corn Bill. Sir Robert Peel, Lord Palmerston, Sir Rowland Hill and Benjamin Disraeli, Lord Beaconsfield, are all remembered on medals struck when they died. Plimsoll, advocate of the 'Plimsoll'

line, to prevent the overloading of ships, is shown with one of the 'coffin ships', in 1875, and the splendid-looking Baron Albert Grant struck a portrait medal on his re-election as MP for Kidderminster.

One might have expected more medals to have arisen from the war in Crimea, but the only souvenir portrait medals are a charming one of Florence Nightingale, by John Pinches, and one of Sir Charles Napier standing on the deck of *The Duke of Wellington*. General Gordon's portrait was taken from a famous photograph in which he wears a fez. The medal was issued to commemorate his death at Khartoum in 1885. The Boer War had many heroes, though few of them became the subject of portrait medals. There is one bearing the imposing name and image of Field Marshal Lord

Many medals commemorated the death of the Duke of Wellington in 1852. This one was struck for the public funeral service at St Paul's Cathedral in London.

Irish politics and history have created their own heroes. Here Daniel O'Connell is suitably robed on this medal by W. Woodhouse of Dublin.

William Gladstone's achievements do not seem to have been the subject of many souvenir medals, but a visit to Leeds in 1881 merited one.

The deaths of famous politicians have always been the subject for souvenir medals; this commemorates Benjamin Disraeli, Earl of Beaconsfield (1881).

The spirit of the Crimean War — before the horrors became apparent — is shown on this medal of Sir Charles Napier struck in 1854 by Allen and Moore of Birmingham. The obverse legend reads LADS, WAR IS DECLARED.

After the horrors of war the image of Florence Nightingale, reading her Bible, and set within a border of the national flora, is most tranquil. The medal, by John Pinches, is not dated, but was issued in 1855.

General Gordon was a hero long before his death, but his slaughter at Khartoum made him in the eyes of the public, and on this medal, THE LATEST CHRISTIAN MARTYR.

Fourteen years penal servitude was the sentence given to the famous imposter, the Tichborne Claimant, in 1873.

The young midget Charles S. Stratton, billed as 'General Tom Thumb' by the showman P. T. Barnum, is shown on a medal in 1844 standing next to an inkstand and eggcup. A less showy medal showed him twenty years later with his wife and daughter.

Roberts VC, but the medal makers probably considered others unnecessary or uncommercial.

Other people who appear on souvenir medals are drawn from a wide range of Victorian activities, amongst them being His Most Serene Highness the Prince of Mantua and Montferrat, who cured 508 people at Greenwich in 1879, and James Morison, the Hygeist, who blamed all disease on impurity in the blood and died (of these impurities?), at the age of sixty in 1840. The British Association honoured John Dalton, the great physicist and chemist, in Manchester in 1842 while in 1843 the Grand Convention of the Friends of Universal Peace recorded its leader, the Marquis de la Rochefoucauld, whose name is virtually unknown today. Sir Marc Isambard Brunel is portrayed on the medals for the opening of the Thames Tunnel in 1843, whilst the portrait of his son, Isambard Kingdom Brunel, is on a medal of the *Great Eastern* issued after

The medical pronouncements of James Morison made him famous in his time, and his death in 1840 was commemorated with a handsome medal by T. R. Pinches.

11

Engineers and pioneers were often the subject of souvenir medals. Sir Marc Isambard Brunel (obverse, left) featured on a number, though his son, Isambard Kingdom Brunel (obverse, above) was never so well honoured.

Sir Joseph Paxton designed the building for the Great Exhibition of 1851, later known as the Crystal Palace.

his death in 1859. Sir Joseph Paxton, who designed the Crystal Palace, took second place to Queen Victoria and Prince Albert on the medals for the Great Exhibition of 1851, but, when the Crystal Palace was moved to Sydenham, Pinches featured him on a souvenir medal. William Dargan, the organiser, appears on the Dublin Exhibition medal of 1853; similarly the wild-looking S. Lee Bapty is on the one struck for the Edinburgh Exhibition of 1890. The youthful General Tom Thumb (Charles S. Stratton), the midget exploited by P. T. Barnum, appears on several medals of 1844, when he was only six and another, struck twenty years later, shows him with his wife and daughter. Blondin, who crossed Niagara Falls on a tightrope in 1860

watched by the Prince of Wales, who was visiting Canada, is commemorated on a medal made in Birmingham. Two famous defendants were featured on medals, the fraudulent Sir Roger C. D. Tichborne, the Tichborne claimant, and John Mitchell, who was sentenced to fourteen years transportation in 1848. The cessation of transportation to Tasmania was the cause of a rare white metal medal struck in 1853.

The cross-section of people featured on medals gives the collector plenty of scope, for they can be collected for who they are and for what they did. If, as is often the case, the name is not familiar, then more enjoyment can be had from a little research and trying to find out all the details.

Pomp and personification are displayed in abundance on the medal struck for the visit of Queen Victoria to the City of London in November 1837. Britannia stands aside whilst the Queen reaches to touch the sword.

EVENTS OF THE AGE

'The Victorian Age' was the name of the Diamond Jubilee exhibition held at Earls Court in 1897, but the title remains the best description of the vast series of events which mostly have nothing in common save that they occurred during the reign of Queen Victoria. Many souvenir medals commemorate events that are connected in some way with the Royal Family, their travels and the visitors they received. Prince Albert initiated the Great Exhibition in 1851, and many other exhibitions were to follow. A wide range of events, both in peace and war, were associated in some way with the Queen and her family, and the medallists always tended to emphasise the royal connection.

When the young Queen was received by the Lord Mayor and the Corporation of the City of London in 1837, William Wyon made a medal with the famous bust that was adapted for the Penny Black postage stamp. The white metal medals struck at the same time were less elegant. There were medals for royal visits to Scotland in 1842 and to France in 1843 — this, a jolly 'hats off' occasion. Medals were also struck for visits to Ireland in 1849, 1853 and 1900 and to Wales in 1889. Louis Philippe of France made a return visit to England in 1844 and in 1855 both Napoleon III of France and Victor Emmanuel of Sardinia made state visits, commemorated by medals.

There were further medals for royal visits to Cambridge, Manchester, Liverpool and Warwick. The Prince of Wales went to Canada in 1860 (the souvenir medals were made in England) and then to the United States of America, where some medals were made locally. These are now scarce. A medal commemorates his return from India in 1872 and others record the many local visits that he and Princess Alexandra made around Great Britain.

The wars of the Victorian age were fought a long way from home and this was probably one reason why there are so few medals concerned with the various battles and actions. There were military and naval awards enough, so perhaps there was no public demand for souvenirs. The novelty of a Chinese delegation in London, following the Treaty of Nanking, was the subject of a medal in 1842. Pinches struck medals commemorating the Crimean War and the pieces for the battles of Alma, Balaclava and Inkerman were sold at the Crystal Palace. Another medal records the death in 1855 of Lord Raglan, Commander in Chief in the Crimea, whilst the peace signed in 1856 was the subject of several white metal souvenirs. Pinches also produced a large medal for the Indian Mutiny in 1857. During the Boer War medals were struck and sold to raise money for charities. The most famous of these was 'The Absent Minded Beggar'. Rudyard Kipling wrote

A double medallion motif was often used, as on this medal for the royal visit to Ireland in 1849. The medal was struck by I. Parkes in Dublin.

In October 1851 Queen Victoria visited the Earl of Ellesmere and was received in grand style at Worsley Hall, before her visit to Manchester the following day. Both events were commemorated with medals. The obverse, common to both, 'borrowed' from the famous Gothic crown designed by William Wyon in 1847.

Queen Victoria also visited Warwick (above) in 1858 (the medal is by Pinches) and North Wales (left) in 1889.

the poem, which was published in the *Daily Mail,* and Spink's struck the medal, using R. C. Woodville's drawing for the design. White metal examples sold for 5 shillings. The second charitable medal was of the S.S. *Maine,* which was sent to South Africa by the American Ladies, Hospital Ship Fund, whose chairman was Lady Randolph Churchill.

Prince Albert proposed the idea for 'The Great Exhibition in London' of 1851 and the souvenir medal makers, who had the opportunity of selling direct to the public made the most of it, for a great number of different medals were struck.

However, W. J. Taylor, a medallist of Little Queen Street, Holborn, London, was the only one permitted both to strike and to sell a medal in the building. Another major exhibition was held in London in 1862 and souvenir medals were struck for plenty of others. Queen Victoria visited the Exhibition of Art Treasures in Manchester in 1857 and the Prince and Princess of Wales feature on the souvenir medals of the fine arts exhibitions held in London in the early 1870s.

The success of the movement to abolish slavery was marked by a medal

The royal visit to France in 1843, to judge from the medal (above), was a very festive occasion. The medallist, Thomas Ottley of Birmingham, used the Orders of the Garter and St Esprit as part of the reverse design. A medal for the return visit of King Louis Philippe in 1844 (left) was less handsome.

The visit of the Italian patriot Garibaldi in 1864 was less official and more political, but still worthy of a souvenir medal.

15

The Great Exhibition of 1851 was the dream of Prince Albert and he features on this medal by Ottley, together with a fine uncluttered architectural view of the building.

Other medals also showed views of the building.

16

A medal for the International Exhibition of 1862 (below) with its original printed card boxes. The boxes are just as interesting as the medals, and collectors should always accept the chance to buy any souvenir medal with its original box or descriptive leaflet.

The Great Exhibition building, now known as the Crystal Palace, was moved to Sydenham. This medal was struck in the actual building in 1866 by W. J. Taylor.

LEFT: *John Pinches struck medals for the battles of Alma and Balaclava, as well as this spirited design for the battle of Inkerman, fought on 5th November 1854.*

BELOW: *The peace treaty for the end of the Crimean War in 1856 produced this very traditional medal.*

ABOVE: *The figure of Victory on this medal for the Indian Mutiny is shown gazing towards JUSTICE in the distant sunshine.*

RIGHT: *'The Absent Minded Beggar' was Rudyard Kipling's creation, and copies of his poem and this medal were sold to raise money for the Boer War charities.*

The abolition of slavery in the British colonies was a long time coming, but the final date set for the emancipation of slaves just fell within the reign of Queen Victoria.

The abolition of the Corn Laws received the royal assent on 26th June 1846. This medal shows Trade prospering, whilst the figure of the Corn Laws lies defeated, falling off the edge of the medal design.

The Shakespeare tercentenary was celebrated in great style, and with a number of medals, in April 1864.

In 1848 a Chinese junk was sailed to England by an enterprising group who exhibited it and the captain, Chun Ah-You, for money. Both he and his junk feature on a number of souvenir medals.

Sporting medals are a rarity, but Hermit won the Derby in 1867, a race RUN IN A SNOW STORM.

commemorating 1st August 1838, the day set for the emancipation of all slaves in the British colonies. The Earl of Powis struck a medal for the celebrations for the return of twelve Conservative members for Shropshire in the 1841 election: designed by T. Halliday, it has a wonderful panorama of the county. At the same election Essex returned only ten Conservative members, but again a medal was struck. The abolition of the Corn Laws in 1846 was the subject of several medals, as was the New Reform Bill of 1867. The splendid sailing ship shown on the medal for the opening of the Birkenhead Docks in 1847 seems to belong to a much earlier age. The voyage of another curious craft, the Chinese junk *Keying*, which sailed from China, up the Thames, and then to Liverpool, is recorded the following year. On 5th August 1858 Queen Victoria communicated with President James Buchanan of the United States by means of the Atlantic telegraph, but the celebrations were mostly in America and it was the Americans who struck souvenir medals. Also in 1858 a medal was struck for a feast in Oldham at which a bull was roasted whole and given to striking colliers. One of the most obscure events for which a medal was struck must have been the thirty-eighth Ditchling Gooseberry and Currant Show and Stoolball Match and Kettle Feast, held in 1860.

Statues were unveiled, anniversaries were celebrated, but sport was not, in any form, a national fixation. There were no medals for the first man to swim the Channel, the first Wimbledon tennis championship, the first cricket Test Match or football's first FA Cup Final. But on 22nd May 1867 the Derby was run in a snowstorm. It was won by Hermit, winning £3,000 for his trainer. The horse and the snow are recorded on a small souvenir medal, no doubt paid for out of the winnings.

PROGRESS AND BUILDING

The Victorian age saw an amazing expansion in industry, engineering, science and building. Today the success of this progress is often measured by the many familiar things that have survived for a century and more. The age is identified with the expansion of the railways, although the railway was a Georgian dream and the first railway medal was issued in the reign of William IV. Medals record a number of the new Victorian railways; indeed the Grand Junction Railway linking Birmingham, Liverpool and Manchester was opened only fifteen days after the accession. This railway and the Edinburgh and Glasgow Railway, opened in 1842, gave the medallists plenty of opportunity for some fine topographical scenes. Curiously, these medals all lacked detailed representations of the engines but in 1855 the South Devon Railway must have made a big feature of an engine at the Bradley Wood Fête, for the attraction was worthy of a small commemorative medal. Another medal shows the three thousandth engine built at Crewe, in 1887. As this was Jubilee year the medal doubles as a Jubilee souvenir. Railway medals feature throughout the reign and there is a white metal medal for the opening of Nottingham Central Station, on the Queen's last birthday, 24th May 1900.

Bridges, too, were often commemorated on souvenir medals. The Hungerford and Lambeth Suspension Foot Bridge was recorded twice, for medals were struck on its opening in 1845 and again when it reopened in 1864, in its new location, as the Clifton Suspension Bridge. The bridge was an early success of Isambard Kingdom Brunel. In 1849 Queen Victoria, aboard the royal train, opened the new bridge between Newcastle and Gateshead, performing the ceremony in the middle of the bridge, to avoid showing preference to either place. The souvenir medal shows a funnel and a puff of smoke from the train on the bridge. The Prince of Wales opened the Forth Bridge in 1890, and the souvenir medal recorded the impressive dimensions and the cost of £3,177,000. Four years later, when he opened Tower Bridge in London, the City Corporation struck a large and splendid copper medal, for which the jolly white metal souvenir was no competition.

LEFT: *The Thames Tunnel was commemorated with a large number of white metal medals. This is the reverse of the medal of Sir Marc Isambard Brunel (page 12).*

BELOW: *Other medals of the tunnel show various views — and the costs.*

Two names that dominate engineering achievement are those of Sir Marc Isambard Brunel and his son, Isambard Kingdom Brunel. The father's amazing career, from French refugee to business entrepreneur, explains some of the determination of the man who designed the Thames Tunnel between Rotherhithe and Wapping, first devising the protective shield within which it could be built. Medals show various aspects of the completed tunnel, its double horseshoe shape giving plenty of scope for a three-dimensional image. A champion of the tunnel was the Duke of Wellington and one of

the humble white metal medal designs commemorating the opening in 1843 was specially struck for him in gold. The Queen and Prince Albert visited the Thames Tunnel four months later and again souvenir medals were struck but only in white metal. Some of these medals would have been given to the crowds that turned up on the day, in much the same way, as 141 years later, commemorative medals were distributed to the public when Queen Elizabeth II and Prince Philip opened the Thames Barrier.

As is so often the way, many buildings

LEFT: *The SS 'Great Britain' was the triumph of Isambard Kingdom Brunel. Ships have a certain appeal that is well depicted and visually pleasing, even on the cheapest souvenir.*

Medals for the Grand Junction Railway, opened in 1837, feature Liverpool's new railway station and some fine views by Thomas Halliday.

The Glasgow medallist S. Woolfield made this medal in 1842 for the opening of the Edinburgh and Glasgow Railway.

The last year of the Queen's life was a busy one. According to this medal, commemorating the opening of the Nottingham Central station on her 81st birthday, she SPARED HERSELF NO EXERTION OR FATIGUE in fulfilling her duties.

A steam locomotive features on the Borough of Crewe's medal for Victoria's Golden Jubilee in 1887.

The Queen opened the Newcastle upon Tyne and Gateshead High Level Bridge on 28th September 1849.

Isambard Kingdom Brunel built the Hungerford and Lambeth Suspension Bridge, which was opened in 1845. It was dismantled so that the railway bridge to Charing Cross station could be built.

The dismantled Hungerford Bridge was re-erected in 1864 to span the Clifton Gorge, near Bristol, where it still stands.

The Prince of Wales opened Tower Bridge in 1894. It has become one of the most popular landmarks in London.

Buildings on medals are usually self explanatory. This commemorates the Sailors' Home in Liverpool, founded in 1846.

The Governesses Benevolent Institution, Kentish Town, London, was opened in 1848.

which now seem to be of little interest or importance were recorded on medals and of the many worthy buildings that have survived to be considered masterpieces by the present generation only a few are the subjects of medals. The collector with an interest in Victorian architecture may well find this an incentive for there is always more attraction in the less common, the more obscure and the unusual. Buildings, or parts of them, feature on a great number of medals: railway medals might show station porticoes, exhibition medals usually show the building in which the exhibition took place. The scope and range is wide. In some the building may be hardly more than implied, as on the medal for the laying of the foundation stone of Saint George's Hall, Liverpool, where the grand front is all but hidden behind a group of personified virtues.

The destruction of the Houses of Parliament by fire in 1834 was not the subject of any medal but the building of the new Houses of Parliament was recorded on several. These medals must have been produced well in advance of the completion of the building, for the views represent Sir Charles Barry's original design and are not at all as the building looked when finished, or indeed as it looks now. Other public buildings featured on medals include the Royal Exchange and the Coal Exchange in London, hospitals and dispensaries, institutions, town halls, orphanages, sailors' homes and even an asylum built for the Governesses Benevolent Institution in Kentish Town, London (which was opened by the Duke of Cambridge in 1848). Of buildings for the amusement of the people, there were medals for the opening of the Alexandra Palace, north London, on May Day 1875, and of the Blackpool Tower in 1891. Even the dead were not forgotten, with medals for the Church of England Cemetery in Birmingham, dated 1848, and for the Leicester Cemetery, dated 1850.

The buildings and monuments shown on these medals serve to show the wide variety of style, but it is comforting that amongst all these serious pieces there is room for some eccentricity, provided by His Highness Ishree Maha Rajah Benares, who built a well at Stoke Row in Oxfordshire and commemorated it, and himself, on a small white metal souvenir medal.

 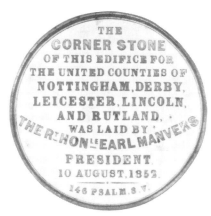

The Midland Institution for the Blind was founded in Nottingham in 1852.

The new Royal Exchange in the City of London was depicted on a number of medals, struck when it was opened in 1844.

The town halls of Leeds, 1858 (top); Chester, 1869 (upper centre); and Sheffield, 1897 (lower centre); together with the public library and museum at Preston, 1882 (bottom); are among those medals of local interest.

ABOVE: *The Alexandra Palace, London's famous 'Ally Pally', was opened on May Day 1875.*

RIGHT: *The Blackpool Tower is a copy of the much taller Eiffel Tower in Paris. The foundation stone was laid in 1891.*

The Maharajah's Well in Stoke Row, Oxfordshire, was the decorative folly of an eccentric, and both he (with his hookah) and it are commemorated on this medal of 1872.

Nelson's Column has become the accepted focal point of London, but medals commemorating the opening ceremony in Trafalgar Square, on Trafalgar Day (21st October), 1844, are now rare.

A SOCIAL RECORD

Throughout the Victorian period the industrial expansion that began in the previous century continued apace, and with it grew a desire for improvements in the standard of living and the quality of life in general. An intriguing and wide range of cheap white metal medals are linked with the social history of the age.

In education children have always been encouraged by the prospect of a reward and prize medals in England date back to the reign of Charles II. Mass production made the manufacture of prize medals easy, though some children were probably disappointed to be rewarded with a white metal medal. Most of these medals were issued by church or grammar schools, though Eton College issued some. Towards the end of the reign the school boards of London and other cities and towns issued punctual attendance medals, often engraved with the recipient's name and with a suspension bar and a ribbon on to which further bars could be added year by year. Sunday schools, too, issued both prize and attendance medals, some even with the legends in Welsh.

The Church of England was less active in the striking of medals than the nonconformist churches. The Free Presbyterian Church of Scotland marked its first Assembly in 1843 and an 1839 medal recorded the centenary of Methodism. On a smaller scale the first Baptist church in Bradford celebrated its centenary in 1853 and the Bishop Ryder Memorial Church in Birmingham was commemorated on a medal of 1838 which now serves as a reminder of the church, which was demolished in 1960. Good clean living was emphasised on the many medals issued by the various temperance socities. The style of the medals varied but most carried the pledge: WE AGREE TO ABSTAIN FROM ALL INTOXICATING DRINKS. The British and Foreign Anti-Slavery Society honoured 81-year-old Thomas Clarkson, a lifetime crusader against slavery, on the medal for their convention, in 1840. General Booth is unnamed on the souvenir medal of the Salvation Army Exhibition at the Agricultural Hall in London in 1896 but there is room to proclaim HALLELUJAH! The dour bust of John Wycliffe is on the

General Booth appeared (unnamed) on the souvenir medal for the Salvation Army Exhibition held in London in 1896.

The Duke of Clarence was the patron of the British and Foreign Sailors Society. He died in 1892 and the words IN MEMORIAM had to be added quickly to the medal before a new obverse — with the future George V as patron — could be made.

Temperance societies flourished and a suitably good family, though distinctly upper class, is shown on this medal — presumably reaping the benefits of abstinence.

The famous preacher Theobald Mathew, THE 'APOSTLE OF TEMPERANCE', is shown on this undated souvenir medal.

Thomas Charles of Bala is shown on this Welsh-language Sunday school medal of 1885.

obverse of the souvenir medal for the centenary of the Lutterworth Tradesmen's Original Benefit Society, struck in 1846. A fine sailing ship features on the reverse, as does another, the *Bacchante*, on a medal for the British and Foreign Sailors Society. The medal was struck in 1892 with the fine uniformed figure of their patron, the Duke of Clarence, on the obverse, but with his death the legend had to be rearranged to include the words IN MEMORIAM.

Most souvenir medals are bought on an impulse of wanting some record of an occasion. A British Museum exhibition in 1979 called medals 'The Mirror of History', for they reflect all aspects of time, place and personalities. The appeal for collectors of medals is in owning an object that forms a link, however small, with a unique part of history. Medals, especially the Victorian white metal souvenir medals, are plentiful and collectable. They may not be quite the 'vocal monuments' that John Evelyn wrote about in the seventeenth century, but in them one discovers a wealth of information. There is pleasure in their study and delight in their ownership.

ADVICE FOR COLLECTORS

There is no single dealer in the United Kingdom specialising only in Victorian white metal medals, but a comprehensive directory of dealers is published each year in *Coins Market Values,* a Link House publication. Many of the dealers who are members of the British Numismatic Trade Association (BNTA) carry commemorative medals in their stock and the larger and longer-established dealers often have a good range of white metal medals which may have accumu-

There must have been a demand for general prize medals, such as this RE-WARD OF MERIT, that could be ordered in bulk by schools throughout Britain.

Robert Raikes, the founder of Sunday schools, features on this medal issued to children as part of the centenary celebrations of 1880.

30

The School Board for London's prize medals for punctual attendance were awarded in great numbers — the Victorian child must have been very punctual. This one uses Bowcher's Jubilee head of 1897 but was issued in 1899.

lated over the years. Most collectors will find that a personal visit to a dealer is nearly always more successful than a protracted postal correspondence. Many antique shops have an odd box kept in the background with a few medals in it, but bargains are seldom found, for when a dealer is uncertain about what he is selling the tendency is to over-price.

No auctioneer would find it worthwhile to sell white metal medals one at a time, but it is well worth scanning the catalogues of the specialist coin auctions for they often contain a few job lots at the end and many an interesting piece may be discovered within them.

Always try and buy medals in good condition, for white metal corrodes easily. Dirty medals can be cleaned with washing-up liquid and a little water but they must be thoroughly dried. Moisture is again a problem if medals are kept in plastic display envelopes, and many medals have survived a hundred years or more in perfect condition only to be ruined by being kept in a plastic album.

FURTHER READING

Victorian white metal medals form only a small category and no book has been devoted to cataloguing them. However, many are listed in two specialist publications:

Brown, Laurence. *British Historical Medals, 1760 — 1960, Volume II, 1837 — 1901.* B. A. Seaby, 1987.
Fearon, Daniel. *Spink's Catalogue of British Commemorative Medals, 1558 to the Present Day, with Valuations.* Webb and Bower, 1984.

This medal for the laying of the Atlantic telegraph was struck in the United States. John Bull greets Uncle Sam with a sparkling handshake: HOW ARE YOU JONATHAN (Jonathan or Brother Jonathan was still the accepted name of the American people). The reply is: PURTY WELL OLD FELLER. HEOW'S YOURSELF.

PLACES TO VISIT

Victorian white metal medals have yet to merit specific display in any of Britain's national musuems although they feature in more general displays. Many museums have local pieces included in their displays. For reasons of security public access to the coin and medal collections of most museums is restricted and appointments must be made in advance to view them. All the museums listed here have white metal medals as a part of their larger collections of coins and medals. Intending visitors are advised to find out times of opening before making a special journey.

Birmingham Museum and Art Gallery, Chamberlain Square, Birmingham B3 3DH. Telephone: 021-235 2834. A large reserve collection from the city where so many of these medals were manufactured.

British Museum, Great Russell Street, London WC1B 3DG. Telephone: 01-636 1555. A wide-ranging collection incorporated in the general run of British medals.

Museum of London, London Wall, London EC2Y 5HN. Telephone: 01-600 3699. London history and School Board medals.

National Maritime Museum, Romney Road, Greenwich, London SE10 9NF. Telephone: 01-858 4422. White metal medals feature in a large general display of naval medals which also includes campaign medals.

National Museum of Wales, Cathays Park, Cardiff CF1 3NP. Telephone: Cardiff (0222) 397951. Medals of both Welsh and British interest.

National Railway Museum, Leeman Road, York YO2 4XJ. Telephone: York (0904) 21261. Medals covering all aspects of railway engineering.

Royal Naval Museum, HM Naval Base, Portsmouth, Hampshire PO1 3LR. Telephone: Portsmouth (0705) 822351 extension 23868 or 23869. Medals of naval interest.

Science Museum, Exhibition Road, South Kensington, London SW7 2DD. Telephone: 01-589 3456. Medals feature in many displays.

Ulster Museum, Botanic Gardens, Belfast BT9 5AB. Telephone: Belfast (0232) 668251 to 668255. Mostly medals of Irish interest.

The following are local museums where white metal medals feature in displays from time to time, or where they are held in reserve collections.

Blackburn Museum and Art Gallery, Museum Street, Blackburn, Lancashire BB1 7AJ. Telephone: Blackburn (0254) 667130.

British in India Museum, Sun Street, Colne, Lancashire BB8 0JJ. Telephone: Colne (0282) 63129. Medals of military interest.

City of Bristol Museum and Art Gallery, Queens Road, Bristol BS8 1RL. Telephone: Bristol (0272) 299771.

Devizes Museum, Wiltshire Archaeological and Natural History Society, 41 Long Street, Devizes, Wiltshire SN10 1NS. Telephone: Devizes (0380) 77369.

Ironbridge Gorge Museum, Ironbridge, Telford, Shropshire TF8 7AW. Telephone: Ironbridge (095 245) 3522.

Jersey Museum, 9 Pier Road, St Helier, Jersey, Channel Islands. Telephone: Jersey (0534) 75940.

Leeds City Art Gallery, Municipal Buildings, The Headrow, Leeds LS1 3AA. Telephone: Leeds (0532) 462495.

Town Docks Museum, Queen Victoria Square, Kingston upon Hull HU1 3DX. Telephone: Hull (0482) 222737.